EL REY OF GOLD TEETH

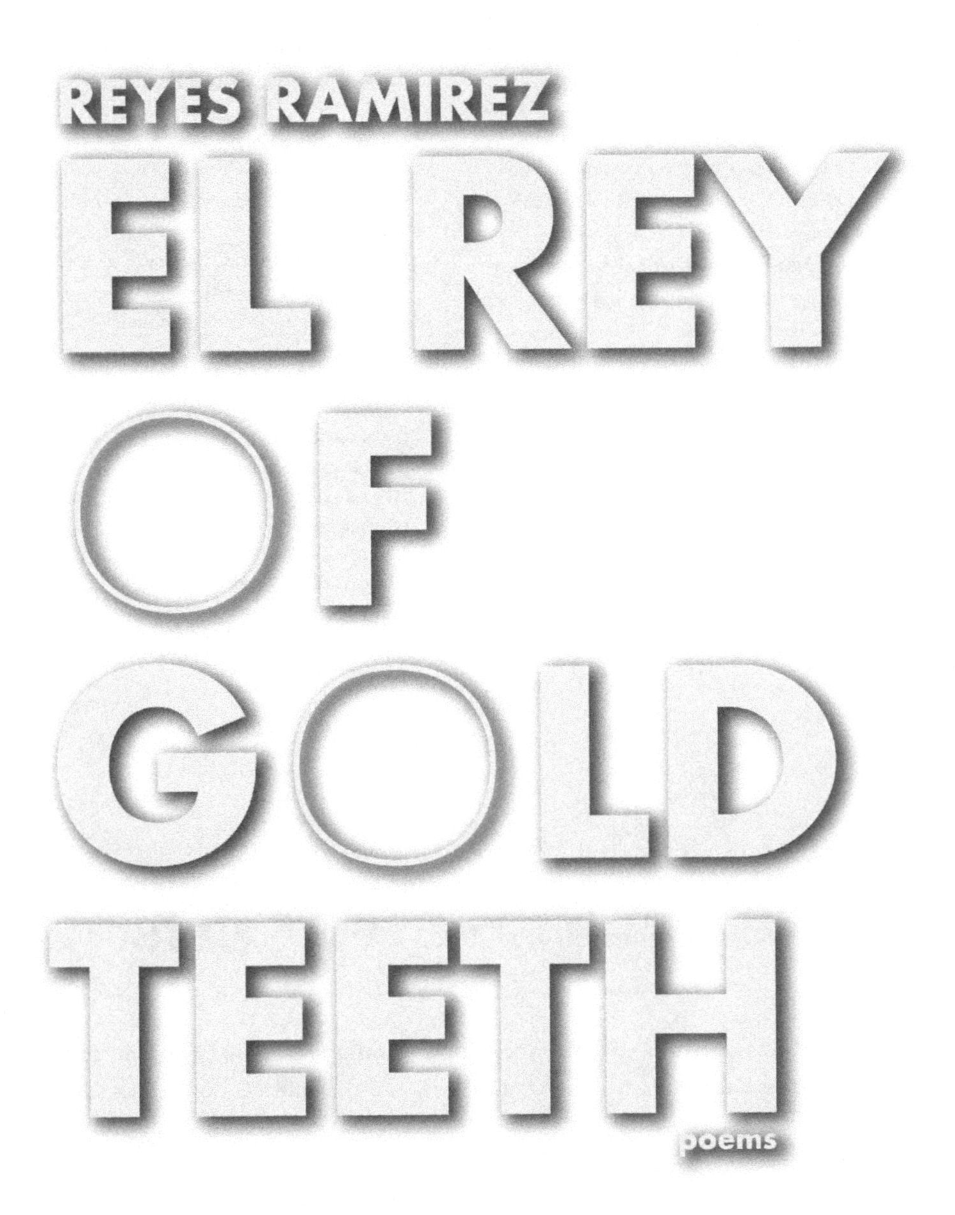

HUB CITY PRESS
SPARTANBURG, SC

Book design: Kate McMullen
Cover Image: Jasmine Zelaya
Author Photo: Romeo Harrell

TEXT: Adobe Garamond Pro
DISPLAY: Futura Condensed ExtraBold

Library of Congress
Cataloging-in-Publication Data

Names: Ramirez, Reyes, 1989- author.
Title: El rey of gold teeth : poems / Reyes Ramirez.
Description: Spartanburg, SC : Hub City Press, [2023] | English, some Spanglish.
Identifiers: LCCN 2023002451 (print)
LCCN 2023002452 (ebook)
ISBN 9798885740197 (trade paperback)
ISBN 9798885740234 (epub)
Subjects: LCGFT: Poetry.
Classification: LCC PS3618.A4645 R49 2023 (print)
LCC PS3618.A4645 (ebook)
DDC 811/.6--dc23/eng/20230224
LC record available at https://lccn.loc.gov/2023002451
LC ebook record available at
https://lccn.loc.gov/2023002452

amazon literary partnership

Hub City Press gratefully acknowledges support from the National Endowment for the Arts, the Amazon Literary Partnership, South Arts, and the South Carolina Arts Commission.

HUB CITY PRESS
200 Ezell Street
Spartanburg, SC 29306
864.577.9349 | www.hubcity.org

CONTENTS

C. A BODY IS EL MAR

D. THE CITY IS EL COSMOS

WHY I LEAVE THE Í OUT

map of a beige texas,
        pockmarked & river-veined
pores labeled into illegibility,
        above a grey mexico
unnamed & clearly partitioned
        by a heart-rate-lined border
made of checks, dashes, of accents,
        of commas, of a strand of hair
dropped from a not-yet mother
        crossing after a not-yet father
who find each other in time to bequeath
        a last name that had been partly lost
in sand, in clouds of running, in gasps,
        in wailing of streams, in the starry pupil
of a panopticon, between the keystrokes
        of a government worker asking
"kay ess two gnome-bray?"
        the response typed quickly, stamped,
next person, the one with a name
        not so demanding & respectful of this
circumstance where your need
        is this country's power.
"you, american without proof,
        what good's a name to you?
we will not recognize it.
        we ask you to move aside &
stand next to the man with a gun."
        the teardrop above a scar,
how can i reclaim
        what i did not shed?

A. EL COSMOS IS A BODY

A LESSON IN POSSESSION

in an egg-shaped room
stale-scented & breathing

a Salvadoran man possessed
sits at a driftwood table

rises calmly unbuttons
his turquoise shirt lined

with names Mauricio
Sergio Belinda etc.

& suffocates it in an obsidian olla
wipes his brow with a knuckle

you ask if the names know your name
the Salvadoran man plucks the shirt

back out as one would snatch
a head by its wiry hair to offer

the smooth of its neck to a knife's
purpose & wrings out ink

that slaps on the bone-white floor
he balls the shirt into a fist

& smears it across a wall
streaks bleeding sap

he drops the shirt the shirt
sighs the shirt se deshace

he points to the floor
then the wall clears his throat

the room exhales his eyes
mirror yours "ahí pues" he says

"read it"

A GOSPEL OF A NEW AMERICA

as translated by its child

1:1 La botella is sacred,
full of alcohol & sueños.

1:2 Remove la botella's cap.
Dispose of it as you would a seed.

1:3 Drink la botella's contents
like one would consume
the cure, you lost perro.

1:4 Your face will swell
with redness, proof
you are still alive.

2:1 La botella is sacred,
unlike you, a vessel
of blood & questions.

2:2 La botella is most sacred
when emptied by tragos
as desperate as a last breath.

2:3 When la botella is empty,
look down the neck as you
would up to the surface
of the ocean as you sink deeper.

3:1 La botella is sacred, conduit of deliverance,
en el nombre del Muerte y del Espíritu Sombrado.

3:2 Bursting love takes years;
la botella is cheap.

3:3 You are not built for love,
solely renewal.

3:4 There are as many botellas
as there are bones resting
under the earth's skin.

3:5 Consume enough botellas
to fill every vein
of your every thought.

3:6 If you consume too much
of la botella, your insides
will spill out & hit the ground
with the sound of an applause.

4:1 La botella is sacred. Through its contents
of alcohol & sueños, you will not feel
the tightening grasp of eternity around
your melting heart.

4:2 There will be better men than you in:
looks, money, personality, strength,
loving, courage, affection, body, soul,
mind, humor, anger, & it will not be fair.

4:3 Every defeat
you must face
alone.

4:4 Everything will hurt;
there is no great love.

4:5 La botella's contents
of alcohol & sueños
will romance these truths
into your bed of clemency.

5:1 La botella is sacred;
the opposite of death
is sex.

5:2 Love the body imperfect.

5:3 Love the body
which welcomes
your pitiful embrace.

5:4 Sex is the union of bodies imperfect,
lustrous with passion, exhales swirling
like smoke from a blue fire, the salt
of your two earths dim on each other's tongue.

6:1 La botella is sacred. Family
& friends make the best enemies.

6:2 Pass la botella onto your offspring
so they too will know these truths.

6:3 When your children discover
the source of your misery,
forget them. Cast them
into the sea of their desires.

6:4 They will not forgive you.
La botella will help you forget.

6:5 You cannot ruin what you
understand.

6:6 To remember is to live in the past;
the past lives to kill the present.

7:1 La botella is sacred
& can never die.
This is not your fault.

7:2 A body dead & a body sleeping
leave the same mark upon the earth.

7:3 Pray they will find
your bones & know who won.

8:1 La botella is sacred
full of alcohol & sueños.

8:2 Your salt will not
nourish the earth.

I. HIJO, PLEASE

Get Ceci. Tell her to gather enough change
to buy manzanas. Make sure they are green.
I want the sourness to overwhelm mi lengua
like the weight of el sol on naked naked skin.

Also, bring me mis pastillas;
It hurts to be angry but feels so good
to be as pitiful as a perro with whittled teeth
and a desperacion to walk on two legs.

Hijo, marry a Mexicana because the desire
for something sweet is natural & mi gente
have understood this desire since they
ripped hearts out of chests.

Pero ya te conozco. You don't like your family,
When I was your age, I was raising my sisters,
So I understand. Míranme ya. You give
everyone everything & you're still sola.

II. HIJO, PLEASE

Speak to gringos como un perrito,
like always starting a love song.
Cuando limpias algo for white people,
do it like they're giving you un favor

by letting you scrub their floor,
fold they clothes, not looking
in their eyes from a corner, lo que sea.
A veces, they will leave cash algun lado,

arriba de un mueble, next to a toy,
by the alcohol, y will check if it's gone.
gringos respect dogs & results.
you are a mexican compromise.

por cierto, whites are un investment,
you get what you need from them
& their childrens' children
y si dices 'yes, thank you.'

A LESSON THROUGH POST-EXILIC FRAGMENTS I

0.

i had a name generations before
my birth: a crown ombréd with rust &
texture of a turtle's shell. i stopped
crying when it heavied my damp head.
my father facilitated this ceremony.

4.

i spoke to my grandfather with my name
over the phone. 'mijo,' he called me as though
he'd held me before. i'd met tíos, & they too
spoke in history. "how many uncles do i have?"
he answered, "estamos en todas partes."

5.

his first piece of advice, hombre a hombre,
came after a spanking for not hearing him
shout stop as I walked away at the store:
'do not cry when you are hurt, or
they will know how to hurt you.'

6.

passed out in his car drunk, he
parked near the bridge. she stopped
waiting up for him after the third time.
her eyes were too burdened by the lull
of canary light. i'd forget how to sleep.

10.

a father boils shellfish, squid, bouillon.
a blue crab pinches a son's arm.
a father teaches a son to lift the crab
by its hind leg, drop it into babbling water,
& watch the shell rose.

12.

because my eyes alone could not translate
reality reliably, she finally calls him after the
optometrist's assistant hands over a thick bill
for my glasses. she could've pulled a trigger
when he asked, "¿que que necesita ver?"

LA PULGA

the fake sapphire
in this iron knife's
brass handle endows
it with an appeal

buying this silver
dollar-sized turtle
is the initial step
in a journey
to atrophy

air so humid
mosquitos
swim to islands
of flesh

it's not a real gun
simply a replica
with implications

every mannequin
with a sombrero
is a father figure

cajeta right here
so sweet you'll shit
marigolds

purchase a fake baseball card & you've inherited a curse handed down by George Washington | he's airbrushed on a jean jacket with Spongebob wearing Rockets colors | they both grin butter over decks of cash aflame

on a series of shirts,
Tweety is a Chicana
Bart Simpson is Dominican
Vegeta is Salvadoreño now

this quarter
from 1897
was found in
my tia's cupholder

porfa diosito, make me
child once more,
that first sip of
choco milk

a bunch of boxes: piles of records next to colanders inside colanders next to a monton de computer paper next to a splatter of keychains from businesses within cities within states within countries next to one-color-off knockoffs of superheroes like Special Man or Sense of Truth League next to rattles of aspirin & acetaminophen next to a child in a lawn chair watching you

on a water-warped
DVD box cover
there's an organ
disappearing
into an orifice

someone's tio is so drunk | he'll confess his love for you | before being carried off the premises | arms limped over a set of hombros

an old woman
finger-picks
an orange guitar
a parrot squawks
of heartache
in Mexican Spanish

on a paperweight, a cartoon man
is fishing waist deep in a lake
while a catfish sucks his cock.
a mug is in the shape of a breast.
the nipple is a peephole.

legally, i can't sell
you these fireworks
but i'm an American
here's ten

here's a copy of Playboy from 1978 | with a white woman pouting on the dog-eared cover | her lipstick's red is what | a generation of gringos thought of during climax | for real

fresas so fresh
you'll kiss my feet

a ferris wheel is yet
another solar system
to a fly
they are here
for the food too

get your elote en vaso
here pon chile,
limon, crema
it won't taste perfect
again

a puppy so cute
you'll crumple
into a storm cloud
of weeping

yes, free car show tonight
the lowriders moan neon blue

beer so cold primo
you'll miss everybody

BEING STUCK IN TRAFFIC WITH MY BIG SISTER ON I-45 S AT 6 P.M. IS MY AMERICA

can the radio play hip hop,
then cumbia,   classic
rock, then pop oblea sweet?

there's   conversations
about a war, then prayer,
swearing, someone asking
why love can hurt so much.

is it cuz
the distance
between wanting someone
& them wanting you back
is so vast,   so great?

i think it's this gulf of yearning,
this   tectonic plate of want,
reminding us   not everything
in short lives can be fulfilled, yes.

& starting anew
takes more life?

oh for sure.   it's static
interrupted by someone speaking
in another language. then silence.
look outside   the car window.

the freeway wall
forms a frame bottom
to an infinite painting.
the sky's a bed of lavender
rusted by dying sunshine.

aren't those clouds up there
actually loose feathers
to a big bird   who takes
people away with too many
questions?

just a graveyard
        of creamsicles.
you're supposed to
hold your breath.

i'm looking equally
at the other drivers.
we all face forward.

is every windshield
a pair of glasses into
a soul's   polyester
interior littered with
    receipts & cups?

every driver's a city
without ordinances
for what's needed.
                        every
car's its own riddle.
like this grey sedan.

look! the bumper has
stickers of a team's
flag   a radio station
that doesn't exist   or
maybe   bible verse?
& one that says *if you*
            can read this, suck my

yes! the bumper is truly
the windowsill
                        to the soul.
the trunk
                        is the soul itself.

now look! in the rear
windshield, a kid plays
with die-cast toy cars
on the back rest.

what a film he composes!
one sleek car races another.
a fire truck crashes
into a spaceship.

there's even a convertible
zig zagging between the
headrests & seatbelt
straps. his mouth
performs explosions.
will i ever be so lucky?

i don't know. maybe
the radio sings through
old men. maybe
the radio speaks in
spanish about
moratoriums. maybe
radio's broken.

still, he's created this
universe of joy within a
city of waiting within
a state of waiting

within a nation of violence
within a continent of theft
within this last world. how
can we not be so lucky? tell
me what's right out
that window?

an atmosphere blotted like
fingerprints on a cake. some
painting continues.
to birds we're rows of
smelly cans & broken glass.

that's good. here's the exit.
this stream of consciousness
tributaries. we're breaking away
from this mind.

were we floating in a river of
concrete, growling engines,
& blood?
first it's hot then
it's too cold. booty
& back so stiff,
i want to be
elsewhere.

well, the world persists
despite our desires.
we're all sitting &
trying to escape our
dead-lined bodies.

how do we achieve what's
next in our destinies?

we enter another sleep. we
won't remember this dream
when we awake.

POZOLE

examine handsome pork & note the vulnerabilities
    the ear's blush, the feet's foggy tendons,
    the ruby pierna's coat of grasa,
    a lightning of white cartilage.
    strip the gummy fat & know
    what must be made bare
place them all in la olla with streaks of coaled tears
    full of agua herviendo.
    what is any sabor but a flesh boiled
        until clouds of loam float
        to the water's screaming surface
        like souls to rapture?
skim the sputtering espuma. add ajos, onion, salt, bullion,
    whatever may grace throat & stomach
      with wax-thick broth.
    a recipe is a litany
      of what has nourished
      the history of your becoming.
    stir so nothing sinks & sticks
open latas of white hominy, handwash them
      like spilled teeth, like nascent pearls,
      like orbs of wisdom
        from the dead.
    continue boiling. continue waiting. continue living.
    remove what can no longer give: cebolla, garlic, doubt.
      add bay leaf. add oregano. add what cannot be said.
taste this labor. taste what's been tasted before you,
    what has provided clarity beyond hunger,
    what has been prepared to the singing
      of those who cannot hear your music,
      by those now in unwakeable sleep,
      through your mother's mother's hope,
      through the instinct to reach across a time
         & say You are here.
Is it possible to ever be alone?

THE FABULOUS WONDROUS OUTFITS OF THE FABULOUS WONDER TWINS

"Everlasting Love," Gloria Estefan, 1994 (2:43)

plumes of lilac paradise birds clench
& the equator echoes purple.
unclaimed oceans of lavender gyre
once, twice, three times
& bamboo trunk sprouts before a mirror.

in some city, buttercream cars quiver
        from drops of violet rain.
in a looted village far away,
a newborn widow prays:
        "may every petunia
        blossom my portrait
        so those lost in fields
        will never be alone"

SELENA'S LAST CONCERT IN HOUSTON

I looked up at the TV
child eyes electric bright
from Selena's jumpsuit
pulled from the purple cosmos
which shimmered across
her great cuerpo of curves—
the arc of the universe bending
to the whim of a Chicana.

Every organ piled in my belly.
I felt the weight of my existence
burdened with potential or defeat
disgrace or love rumbling enough
to bring me to my knees in prayer
or mercy, dazed in awe or reverence
as she sang 'flor' then composed one
out of the black air with her hand
as though casting with bendiciones.
She will soon receive a gunshot
in her shoulder, infinite potential
spilling like water out of a tipped pitcher.
Whatever beauty there is they want it
for themselves oh so scary fast.
We shouldn't fear what's greater than us
lest we never leave our bodies
because at 23, Selena sang into a void
and demanded a response—
left hand across her breasts, breathing in
through a smiling boca pulses
of screaming amor.

For a moment of eternity, she looked
into the camera through her bangs,
disordered by wild performance
at me, alone, just sitting there draped
with a blanket in the shadow-dancing
living room of my mom's apartment.

ASTHMA ATTACK

<table>
<tr><td>the wet of
this house</td><td>my coughs
a rubber ball</td><td>flood
bouncing</td></tr>
<tr><td></td><td colspan="2">on sand</td></tr>
<tr><td>Mom
I could breathe</td><td>placed me
in my sleep</td><td>in two chairs &
I sat in one as</td></tr>
<tr><td></td><td colspan="2">a proper man</td></tr>
<tr><td>at dinner
like a casket</td><td>the other held
I tasted cold</td><td>my child feet
wind</td></tr>
<tr><td></td><td colspan="2">scraping knees</td></tr>
<tr><td>every inhale
gunked up</td><td>scorched with oil
bayou water at</td><td>every exhale
the curve of</td></tr>
<tr><td></td><td colspan="2">my windpipe</td></tr>
<tr><td>I was told
I'd never met
the bus</td><td>I resembled
a face drooped like
in an ambulance</td><td>an uncle
a drunk on
fast</td></tr>
<tr><td></td><td colspan="2">as a scream</td></tr>
<tr><td>in the night
my nose & lips</td><td>a plastic mask
by then</td><td>palmed
my breath wheezed like</td></tr>
<tr><td></td><td colspan="2">cicadas</td></tr>
</table>

singing in	the jaws of	summer
I dreamt	a balloon	groaning

from expansion

Death is	a smoothbore	funnel of light
each lung	narrows into it	hissing

like searing beef

finally stabilized	in a hospital bed	the next morning
my mom asked	when I could leave	doctor said now
now look right	here	boy

I turned my head

to see	out the square	windows
& the sun's	a glass piñata full	of honey stuck

in a tree

III. HIJO, PLEASE

Vete a la tienda. Comprame esas tarjetitas
to call your tías, tus tíos. Dicele al señor,
'señor, quiero tarjetas pa llamar mis tíos,
mis tías en mexico.' Quick, please.

No sales así. Try to look presentable,
like you have a madre that buys you clothes.
Te lo juro, god is a mother. Who
else loves what grows to forget you.

If there's cambio, no seas malo,
buy la viejita que reza porfa
something dulce. Que cruel la vida is.
Mijo, tienes que ser buena gente.

When you marry, love your wife. Kiss
her hands every night antes de dormir.
You never know. Ama tu gente. Be kind
or Diosito will make you kind.

IV. HIJO, PLEASE

Entiende que all times es hard.
Los malos siempre estaran in charge,
y los buenos sobreviven.
What can you do? If you love

god, you surrender what you
love most to him. Y si no confias
en la justicia, no existe. If justicia
is not true, que estamos haciendo.

Esa cara. I hate when you remind me
of tu padre. Have some hope. Hazme algo.
Promise me que nunca tomarás. You father,
his father, his father father, alcohólicos.

I know what's wrong with you,
but I cannot fix it. Es tu curse.
Los dos pueden ser verdad: el nunca
estaba aquí & you're just like him.

A LESSON THROUGH POST-EXILIC FRAGMENTS II

17.

over the phone, he finally told me
what happened to him as a boy.
i'd already been that age, which passed
me like a late bus. i was too afraid to ask
for details. our breathing kindled the line.

18.

a father & son listen to a sermon sitting
in folding chairs at a halogen-lit church in
a shopping center. 'god is the hand, you
are the tool,' a woman in a blue-white gown
says. the father weeps into his palms.

20.

a father survives a car wreck in Georgia
after his late shift at the packinghouse.
the lamppost uprooted like a molar from
a dog's mouth. they said his body was so aloof
from drink, he broke a bone. the crown chipped.

21a.

the last time we meet, we visit his side
of the family. he couldn't lift his arms
much so we hugged around our waists.
i met new tios & tias, primos & primas,
tio Sergio's crown stormclouded but clean.

21b.

his last piece of advice, which he didn't know
was his last, i think was, "live a good life. no seas
como esos que lo gasten en mujeres y alcohol."
over breakfast, my tios & tias said i have his hair
& eyes. they snap our picture. we didn't blink.

B. THE CITY IS EL MAR

PUPUSAS

the pupusa is a portrait
        of an honest earth.
                the coarse burns continents,
        the auroral dough a sea.
water joined masa through tumult
        & sphered, flattened then crowned,
                filled with meat & milk then smoothed,
        heat birthed & bitten.
no, the pupusa is an homage
        to the laborer's backhand
                where scars simmer & settle,
        strawberry skin browns.
sweated flesh crackles on steaming metal,
        grease singing smoke loud then sweet over & over,
                flipped & rested, an iris weepy then dry,
        ashen islands form & a back stiffens.
no, the pupusa is a documentation
        of every pecado,
                the taut pink palate
        a receipt for indulgence.
a sheet of young wood pulp dims,
        then an emergence of weighty shadows.
                a sycamore pith rises & splits
        & spits a globe of queso.
no, the pupusa is a bulging mirror
        to this sleepless face. examine
                the wrinkle bowls under each eye & find
        another tired eye under another tired eye.
the cream sol bulges then sombers,
        sunspots & scabs black;
                what can this light nourish
        but a body ripe with eonic exhaustion?

no, the pupusa is a portrait
    of this life, crusting & breaking
        with every lick & tooth, the desire & gift
    of jarabe yielding to the shape of a belly.
crack open the soft disc egg
    & study its ivory thick blood & tender marron,
        stretching like a timeline of grief,
    & lap the fresh veins.

LA ALONDRA DE LA FRONTERA

for Lydia Mendoza

I.

I lay down in a park. "A wanderer must constantly search for themselves or become a victim of circumstance," I hear the birds sing to each other on the branches of dying trees. I've also heard this in the running of water, from the etches in bathroom stalls, the stretch of a father's smile, the smoke from a match, in the scratching pills do against the walls of their bottle, from my reflection every night before work. A hair falls from my head & into the grass.

II.

In a room out of the thousands she will play in her life, Lydia Mendoza picks up a guitar & strums twelve strings with her eyes closed, dizzy with love and reverberation. She wears a huipil and skirt the color of reds, greens, yellows, oranges, blues and white but her songs will be of dark hearts, dark doves, dark betrayal, dark tangos, dark death, dark ojos, bad men, bad lives, bad jealousy, cruel fates, and cruel, bad, dark love. The music from her guitar will resonate through the air as though bleeding to death. Listen and feel the sun setting in your heart.

III.

Imagine yourself anywhere. How long do you get to feel at peace in one place before its pieces remind you that nothing lasts? The water in a jug, the couples sitting together, the story in the book in your hand, the food on a plate, the cleanliness of a floor, the song playing right now, the one sun above you, each strand of grass holding me up in their prayer to the sky. "Wandering is simply one life entering another," the grackles sing to their hungry chicks.

IV.

I've lost jobs, friends, lovers, parents. A feeling you get after is how long you have yourself before time claims that too. La Alondra picked up a guitar at twelve years old and never stopped. How does one sing for 79 years? How does one dedicate their life to wander from place to place for so long, planting trees of dark beauty for other songbirds to nest in? I know no music. Lydia Mendoza, if I give you my voice, will you teach me to sing?

V.

Even a good song must end. Even a bad life finishes its cycle. La Alondra de la Frontera understood this with each piece that she sang as though almost breaking into tears or laughter. What is a song other than a life? If a song is a life and a life is a song, then how many songs can one sing in a life? How many lives can one live in a song? Can a song exist to respond to others? Can a song be built on the foundations of another? "Love must be repaid with love, or else or it is all a lie," the soaring birds warble down at those who walk.

VI.

Imagine walking into a dark room with a spotlight fixated on a chair upon the stage, sitting down, drinking beer fast enough to feel its ice coldness settle in your stomach and hear La Alondra de la Frontera strum her guitar whose vibrations say: "Tell me your sadness & give me your berrinches, your lagrimas, your grief, your pecados, your fears, your pains, your tristesas so that we may sing them together."

VII.

A songbird has no purpose but to sing. Anything else is in service to the song: eating, flying north or south, laying an egg and hatching it, feeding hatchlings and teaching them to fly, to be songbirds themselves. Each blade of grass stands in its own length. Each tree its own number of branches. No two songbirds sound alike.

V. HIJO, PLEASE

You were always el más feo.
Everyone else in the family is gorgeous,
beautiful Mexicanos with blue blue eyes
that could pass off as europeos.

I give birth to you y tu padre gets all the credit.
Your cheeks tan gacho as if you were melting
eyes vacío como bones
que barbaridad que asco que lastima.

As my body lies dying, cortame el pelo,
all of it, take it to Mexico,
throw it into a gust so mi alma
fades like miel into milk

Make sure my body is put in fire
so that my skin does not rot
yellow like the shell of a chicharra
that can be crushed between dedos.

VI. HIJO, PLEASE

¿Estás enojado? For calling you feo?
Pues, madres have to be honest.
I can tell you, ay, you're so perfect
& beautiful, pero I'd be a liar.

How can I give you to the world
if you don't know how it's going
to treat you? I cannot teach
my son to die afraid, oigame.

You give a flower too much water
y se muere. You give your heart
to someone y they disappear. You give
everything of yourself, hasta que te mata,

y se olviden. If you love somebody,
you can accept the little cruelties.
If you can't do it for me, then who?
Mi feo, mi gordo, mi vida.

A LESSON THROUGH POST-EXILIC FRAGMENTS III

23a.

i'd drank so much gin i could not speak.
i laid in a broken bed at the edge
of a spinning room. i'd thought about how
biting into a shell will splinter it, how
ingesting the pieces could shred intestines.

23b.

beer-warm sweating & vodka bottle deep,
i limp around my apartment like a haunting.
doesn't everyone become their father
when their hair covers their eyes,
wearing jeans with a tight belt?

24.

a call in the night from his new partner
was how i learned he returned to drinking.
"will you speak to him?" she asked.
when i dialed, there was no answer.
i've never changed my number.

EDDIE GUERRERO ENTERS A RING HOLDING THE WORLD CHAMPIONSHIP

the body brown, belt gold, eyes closed, nose in the air,
shoulders shake to each word: i lie, i cheat, i steal.

white men, what you hold sacred we will take: money, cars,
liquor, land, life, winning. you won't like this. that's fine.

this world champion drives bouncing low lows, talks shit.
i: grin through crimson masks, slit roaring red, red rain;

lift bodies into orbit, drop them like judgements;
leap from turnbuckles, bronze fist blooming into flames.

brown bodies know that violence is the marriage
between their hot ambition and the rule of law.

what respect can i have for the word 'legal' since
'illegal' can describe our skin, our joy, our life?

i lie, i cheat, i steal. i lie, i cheat, i steal.
this champion of the world pokes eyes, low-blows, spits.

behind the ref's back, i hit the floor with a chair
(metal clang), chuck it into my opponent's hands,

collapse as though just shot. the ref turns around, shocked.
i point to my white foe, get them disqualified.

there's no difference from a fair win and a win
except how much your faith in the system frees you.

what good are your rules if they grant only your dignity?
what good are your codes if broken by our breathing?

this world champion struts over a white body.
we're not meant to exist with such extravagance.

i lie, i cheat, i steal. we lie, we cheat, we steal.
smile with your tongue out in celebration of broken laws.

THE FABULOUS WONDROUS OUTFITS OF THE FABULOUS WONDER TWINS

"Vertigogo," Combustible Edison, 1995 (00:45)

everything has a twin, linked by invisible umbilical cords,
& everything must meet its twin before completion.

old hands with veins full of blue blood trace
the lightning blue rivers on a once-lost map.

a brown child's silver eyes marvel
under chrome light from a brown box.

the knife scales of a catfish break a mud-water
surface & rhinestone under a Southern sun.

what is to be said of what must be overcome?
the machine of your nation's history can stall,

& the sweetness of mantequilla clouds in sunlight
replaced by smoke metastasizing from an ignited car.

consider a wondrous blue nimbus, poofy & hair-like,
spitting down two braids hanging like constant tears;

it rests on a head attached to a body wearing this dress:
equally blue but striped white, the skirt hoops and hoops,

blue-white striped hoops on hoops, each diameter vaster
than last, a sonic boom of fabulous blue in reverse so loud

i cannot hear the limitations of any one body.
here it is happening twice.

imagine fulfilling your completion
twice every living day.

EL SALVADOREÑO AMERICANO AS DECOLONIZER, 1929-1936

for George Meléndez Wright

ive spoken to the surfbird, los arboles verdes, con los coyotes, with los elk in return they said listen for we will say this once listen listen to totuya la última de los Ahwahneechee for the elder will reveal what the white men do what it feels like to return home and see nothing as it was see home as an entirely new land that will need you to point to its hurt and know how to heal it how to love it how to be its child you will not know any of its significance how anything she will say will be of use to you until your people too will be displaced by death by knife by blood by fire by the guns of the very people you work for by the very people who will not see the horror of their ways remove your people after they have made this land their new home remove your people from this very land you have fed loved cared for that is not theirs listen listen listen totuya la última the elder will speak in english spanish the language of the Ahwahneechee and tell you the history of your people before it will come to pass totuya la última the elder the giving will call her people as you will need to even if none will heed your call you fool you lover of lo que es verde you who are doomed totuya la última the elder the giving will not do this for you for she will be healing herself her soul her people so you must listen listen listen so i listened and Totuya indeed said as they said provided me an answer to a question i do not know yet i gave her water looked into her eyes held her hand as she spoke of the beauty of the earth and of her gente how the white man came and started fires that displaced her gente and how the tisayac stood there as it had millions of years before and millions after let her heal the way she needed to i have promised to look after her people's land to cure it from the white man's hand full of garbage and bullets the white man's imagination that emboldens itself to believe it owns everyone else's body and dirt and mind and death and i will speak to the trees, esos árboles verdes, con los coyotes, with los elk osos and ask them what hurts how to cure them how to convince the white man to stop i will help them to stop killing los árboles verdes los coyotes and hope that maybe just maybe los wildflowers will tell me what will befall my people and if anything i do for the land will save mi gente or if at least i can try and make right what the white man has ruined here ruining will ruin and do my best to teach my america to love itself teach the world to love itself dedicate my one life to teach all to love the land let that be enough to stop the onslaught of history of the bullet the blood the knife the fire it must be enough to stop what's coming what else can i give to stop what has happened happening will happen let it be enough please please please porfa porfa porfa

A BROKEN RED-EARED SLIDER'S SHELL

[m.1.]

house de flesh y hueso
glides about un azure womb
skyed con marbled
membrane struck numb
por prisms que shatter
y skitter.

[p.9.]

on hollow log turtle lolls
over another arms y legs
spread out en sacrifice al sun
what does un turtle say al other?
do they search por redness y discuss
what un lake means? what does un turtle
think of el dead tree they rest upon, eyes
closed y body still? does el turtle look
por the redness del dead tree's ear
y whisper to it as well? el turtle y
el dead tree rest as one.

[m.3.]

the one purpose
en this one life es to pack
oneself warmly. Blood
de cold syrup y sand,
everything not radiant
hurts. el sun heartbeats
ceaselessly. there will
be no hurt.

[v.2.]

un ocean still enough por reflection
until green peeks through
shivering on top de vast skin
a seed de flesh y bone inches out
como islands three hundred
million years ago
un island rests upon another island
until plates shift   un island falls
into water, floats away,
amasses moss.

[p.3.]

hay two skies
one shudders over
water. one curves above
cosmos. a plane moans
of death in-between

un stone de flesh y bone
yearns from un blue
plane to rest in star fever

[m.5.]

why are you
tan averse a
submerging tus
hands en
bubbling mud?
por running
tu nose
along flakes
de bark?
shell es made
de mud y bark.

[p.1.]

en captivity
attempt knock over
fixtures they placed
por comfort heating lamps
water filters plastic plants
kick rocks
claw hasta infinity

worm floats
en water open
beak un yawning baby
y ingest offering.

turtle
lays eggs
leaves

[m. .]

[v.3.]

beak nostrils neck plates
a mountain range
top of shell un map
of earth when un island
traced with claw at time
of creation scutes legs
nails eyelash thin el turtle flits los cheeks
of a submissive como casting
un spell de tenderness y power
tickle from a dream
about the snap of a beak
named por el color
el red inherited
from the earth's center
& blood eye
of fresh wounds

[.5.]

cada shell holds
38 fragments of   earth
a body surrenders   heat y
nourishes   rebirth
carapace y plastron
y scute gather as ruins of

[p. .]

look upon   sun stupor
wings de scale y claw
lush mirror de keratin
rubies made   scars
un kaleidoscope folds
y disappears into flight
you   irrelevant

[c.]

en four million
years   they
will find specks
of our imago y
empty shells
of todos turtles

VII. HIJO, PLEASE

Repeat to me what the lady say.
Hija de su chingada madre. Pero
mira. Tratas los gringos con respecto
and they're still like that.

I get it. I'm in their country.
But you American like her. She
supposed to respect you.
Tell this gringa you want los jeans

la de arriba. When she done, digale
you don't want anymore, que you want
las de abajo, so her knees or back
will hurt tomorrow

& she'll have to explain to her childrens
que sometimes things hurt y tell them
que no hay nada que you can do to stop
hurt from coming to them too.

VIII. HIJO, PLEASE

Me voy & I'm not coming back.
The American air tastes like mierda,
not fit to morir in because I've experienced
peace once and was not so aburrido

as these people think, tirando bleach everywhere
y drinking wine that smells like culo.
Yo quiero pain that I've earned,
salvation in the blood under mis uñas.

Mi madre collected: seashells, bracelets,
and nunca killed her chickens. Anything
as long as it could be destroyed.
I want to go home.

I don't care for the violence.
Yo soy la violencia.
I return to it like
a wave back into the sea.

SAL DEL MAR ON BROWN SKIN | A LANGUAGE LOST IN SAND

salt dampens the sand
    where i rise.
i'm a man of the sea.

i've licked clean the eyes
    of charred fish & rub
my thumbs on
    ocean's grit.
i've stood at the coast at night,
    a black screen with no reflection,
& saw the death of my ego.
    the sun smolders my skin
like heartache grafting onto a heart.
    i find no enemy in its light.

—

gulls sky babble & sandpipers
    beak-stab wet sand.
they scatter across beachhead
    as the ocean's many hands clasp
more & more of the coast's neck.

left behind are coral fragments,
    tufts of ripped net, floatsam
of a one-hundred-year-ago war.
    the hermit crabs tossed
upon the shore are torn
    from their borrowed
white shells by yellow beaks.
    i, too, am a mass of messes.

by that, i mean that when
    wooden shards wash up

from a home or a boat
    or a toy or a bed,
i point & identify parts
    of myself.

—

along the hemispheric plane's
    turquoise edge, specks of the living
blot like seagull knees:

a barge, or the memory of a barge,
    meditates on the existence of flesh;
skimmers skim the sea line,
    needles threading invisible string
through trembling velvet;
    oil rigs, or the remains
of ancient cities picked clean
    as a whale fall,
materialize like faces
    in a fever dream.

there, a swimmer's head haunts
    the horizon, a punctuation
bobbing about a sentence
    with no ending.

—

sheets of fish bones & rice grains / shatter on the shore / hissing like rind in aceite / skin sun-kissed / into a surface of mars / if not god then / the sun humbles / a body / sweating tequila & tears / which the sand absorbs / like water / like blood / you won't find answers here / just culled results / the best i can do / is tell you to / imagine closing your eyes / in a rocking boat / & never waking / where you first slept / there's sand in your genetics / niño / lungs lined with silt / barnacles beneath that piel / seawater in the blood

—

the real question is:
what hasn't sand
gotten into?

an ant carries a clump
of beach sand
back to his colony.
the queen asks,
"what can be made
with this?"
no one responds
with, "a home."

yet, the beach membrane
is percolated
with ghost crab air tunnels
that spout breaths
under a slab of seawater.

my mother told me
that if you
love someone,
write your names
in the sand &
let the ocean gather
the scrit into its eternity.

—

sea-mist smothered structures
lining down la playa's spine
are specters of themselves already.
the ocean speaks
of disassemblage.

i've looked into the ocean's
  blue-on-blue horizon
& witnessed desire;
  i wish the world's lines
were currents washing
  upon shores
mercury silver to melt,
  nighten & recede.

—

when driving across a bridge,
  sunlight will alchemize the road
into sea or sky; pray
  whatever deity deems this
return the asphalt's physical property
  lest the car veers into a state
of thrumming silence, an eternal
  contemplation of living or dying.
assume nothing ever drowns.

why yes, i contemplate my passing
  slow like an ocean drowning,
a birth in reverse where i'm anchor-pulled
  into an abysmal unbecoming.

when i'm unafraid, it's even slower.
  during an after-storm hush,
the road is a river of smoke, homes
  renounced & flooded up
to the bed-sheets in a room where
  i've been sleeping for years.

i'm a man of the sea.
  i lay wherever
the soil diamonds with salt.

C. A BODY IS
EL MAR

FINDING KITTENS AFTER A TROPICAL STORM IS MY AMERICA

clouds weep so much   a city can't drink anymore
streets turn into rivers   buildings are a shelter or not
i survey around my home   every surface bloat with wet
choirs of drips dive from branches   they barely mask the mews
pitiful as pennies dancing in a palm   i locate them by pausing breath
listening beyond speaking water   & find hardly more than fetus
edgeless mouth struggling to squeak   raw pink paws thrash again
for nipples on rusted air conditioner   making sense of our paradigm too
body so light not even a shadow   no depression in the damp dirt
underneath the plump belly   when i lift its body in my hands
i cup flesh to kindle heat   for the others, i repeat my process
hold breath, stay still, attune   a mew, step into its ghost, again
they've scattered themselves   into points on a map of disorder
clouds murmur as i collect them   not too far, a kitten is stuck
between a tree trunk & house   one has its noodley leg caught
in the web of a veiny root   the furthest screams at sweating grass
the last i find too late   surviving is a matter of circumstance
homes sip rain or inundate   a man drenches in a 2-ton truck
a kitten remains dry by a tree   their limbs torsion like tired salmon
i clump their bodies   one sucks the foot of another
furry kidneys gasp as a lung   i leave them alone for now
their mother may be hunting   to return & feed them bellyfuls
my presence is a counter spell   yes, a mother may return or be dead
it's counting intricacies of tragedy   that inspires a profound thirst
the logic of abandonment happens   think full storm drain & engulf
to see lines of silver &   consider who are in cages
a tree has toppled   made boat by currents
kittens smush into each other   groaning like a house straining
against the anger of gusts   their eyes will not open
for another week   their ears will remain folded

for a few days more   the only sound is water
falling into water   the only sight is every surface
bound with water   every smell infected
by the specter of water   i dream of awakening on
a brown raft floating about   an alabaster nebula
when i check them next day   i dig a wet hole behind my wet house
with my wet hands   & bury them together
i'll hear mews in door openings   instinctually
in hissings of faucets   i lay on my back
              & become their evidence

THE CHICHARRA

trilling from
the secret limbs
of coronary trees
for drink, heat
& desire are
our mutual oppressors.
the waxy hands of Houston's air
cup our bodies
as though guarding
the last ember from
the last fire.
oh how it would
feel to strip my skin
from the maize-yellow meat
underneath, spiraling
vapor escaping.
a lid sliding off the pot's
rim gargling
honeycomb tripe,
snakeskin empapado
with fever sweat.
i've often mistaken
their mustardy exoskeleton,
abandoned like a truck
snuffed by weeds
along a highway,
for living things.
how could i?
i'd leave my ghost behind,
too, if the rest of me climbed
a tree to ululate
my frothing organs
into the sky's tongue.

if your song were translated,
would i be able to name
the color grains embody
in a heaving field
as sunlight died,
rebirthed, glowered, &
died again? i look up
at a branch.
my ears echo
with the desire
to scream & not be seen.

A 4TH GRADE DANCE PARTY IN A CAFETERIA AT 1 P.M. IS MY AMERICA

children
file in with fluorescent sneakers
chirping across a blue-grey chess
board. adults are all at work.
i chaperone. lunch
ladies load tired pennies
into cylinders. a man
mops a corner. gym teacher
queues a clean playlist.
no child must do anything
except what music inspires.
mira, this barely lit dance
is a nation of motion. i lean
against a wall & be its facilitator.
a scheduled bell rings. the children recognize
one song, then another. those who know how
form a mass & sway to the beat of a 90s hit.
more children join in this stewing of joints
& sound knowing their dances like the milly rock,
the juju, running man. even ones before
their birth like the macarena, wobble, cha-cha slide.
each child becomes another. these must be inherited
languages since movement has been our truth.
i witness a song's lyrics progress until words
everyone has memorized plays. children sing
in one mind from many voices. i need not
be a member of this congregation to be saved by it.
the next bell rings. the children have grown
with ache & understand things end prematurely.
a song, a dance, this nation. the adults continue
their labors. i file children back into a line.
lunch ladies remove their hairnets.

that man mops that corner. gym
teacher is just a gym teacher. we go
back to class & learn math or
science or a history. in the face
of what needs change in this
country, i'm still a
child.

IN THE SIX KILLINGS OF NAZIS BY MACARIO GARCIA, THERE IS A LINEAGE

1519

An ink tide flickered jaguar eyes,
& washed me clean to my bones.
Then I flew into sky until I suffocated;
the sun replaced me with me again.
Here, fire is all there is to drink;
I imbibe enough to become my shadow.
Now, the mountains weep so much blood
my lungs bloat with boiling clay.
When I was pulled from dirt this time,
my skin goldened & settled copper.
When a man sown in iron approached,
I drove a dark rock into his pale neck.

1944

In honest spirit of ending a war,
I gift you one grenade, then another.
May you embrace the shrapnel's many arms
& find peace in death or hurt. Either one.
Every single weapon formed to ruin
bone, sinew, soul & muscle shall prosper
like a lover's kiss on a lover's shoulder
en estos manos míos against you.
These wounds leaking my blood exist, claro,
but when the question becomes, "who lives?
these gringos or this Mexican?" Pues,
the end of my rifle begets answers.

1916

How do you say *I'm sorry* in English?
I want to be sure I forget it. How do you
say *I shot them in their sleep because I like*
to think I've trapped them in a nightmare?
I'm kidding. It was because I was drunk.
I'm kidding. You named this town what?
The nights here are darker than my asshole,
so my friends & I lit fires with wood borrowed
from your homes. You wouldn't understand.
I think I heard that I'm to be tried and hanged?
Well, that's just how it goes sometimes. Like
they say in the good book, me now, you in a bit.

1944

Hijole, look at these machines you've built
for my annihilation: air-cooled, belt fed, open
bolt, recoil operated, steel alloyed, twelve
hundred rounds a minute. They are made
well, but not like me. Please let some kind
of record show: the blonde skin of gringos
is pierced by bullet like child fingers through
cold lard. Astounding how those with piel tan
debil try so hard to convince me it isn't. In Texas,
signs say, "No dogs, No Blacks, No Mexicans
Allowed." In Germany, you speak of some master
race. I've not seen a body more accepting of holes.

1918

Lulled to my knees by the sun's heartbeat,
a gun's lips peck my spine into walking further
with the others, dragging their feet out of step
along a road that ends in a winged dust.
They separate men & women then children.
"My mother believes their luscious blood sings
when sizzled with dirt & sweat," a soldier says.
Another directs me to stand by a cliff
deeper than all of us combined. They ask
what I've done for this country, & my mouth
numbed. When I know what to say,
I'm interrupted by a heavy sleep. *Nothing.*

1945

There's no such thing as water in a cotton field,
only clouds full of salt. When someone passed out,
we asked the sun to be considerate. The whites
spray pistol smoke yet are disgusted by the smoothness
of our hands. There's no such thing as sleep in rows
of beds filled with sunburnt bodies, only alertness.
When someone grieved for all their skin peeling off
like corn husk, we asked our brains to stop taking
in so much detail. It isn't fair to remember everything.
Once, a white man paid us on time with a smile.
"When whites are kind, they're saving up for a cruelty.
It's why you should never weep for any of their dead."

THE FABULOUS WONDROUS OUTFITS OF THE FABULOUS WONDER TWINS

"If It Makes You Happy," Sheryl Crow, 1996 (2:02)

2 obsidian statues pose
during a dull-gold dusk.
they mimic one another
about 2 rhino horns apart:
leaning sideways, hand on hip,
arm teapot stretched.
they both look forward,
not at each other, &
once will their heads turn

to face their 1 face at each other
for as long as 2 guitar strums
then back. their 1 life ends
as the dull-gold dusk darkens
its 1 of many lives across a horizon,
smoke filling an aquarium.
the 2 obsidian statues bleed out
a desperate night through their skin
& become 1 memorial for all sleep.

A LESSON THROUGH POST-EXILIC FRAGMENTS IV

27a.

in a sun-lit classroom full of children sitting
at their desks, i announce, 'a poem is a life. you
have a pencil.' a child asks, 'what exactly
is a poem?' i wave my hand across
the landscape of their sleepy faces.

27b.

i eat a mariscada, a copy of the ocean
swollen with plumped bodies
or a golden pasture with stones & prawn.
whenever mexicans question what i am,
i tell them. they ask how that happens.

28.

a Selena shirt. *viva la raza*. a flag of aztlán.
when i say mexicans & mexican americans
make money from separating kids
from their parents, too, they tell me
that doesn't count.

29.

Both can be true: someone was never here,
& you're just like them. Both true: be
of somewhere & never been. Both are true:
contribute to something & it erases you. One
can't be true: to want me here & it be my fault.

30.

i dreamt i was a crab, & it's right
as i'm boiled. above, i see a face
blurred by the breathing surface
of brine. i'm consumed with red wine.
i awake. my crown is still there.

IX. HIJO, PLEASE

Look en la computer esa chingadera
a song de cuando fue niña. Se va
ponme mi vestido negro. We used to sing
it antes de dormir. Mi mama & me.

Te digo, she want to be a singer
cuando ella fue niña. Sabias que I sing
this song when you baby?
You couldn't sing, but you watched.

Eres como yo. When you love somebody,
you love them con todo el dolor de tu corazón.
When I dic, my heart will stay
even after my bones are rock.

Our curse is we will not be loved
igualmente en como amamos. Hice
lo mejor that I can contigo. Si dios quiere,
you'll love without having to always forgive.

X. HIJO, PLEASE

I don't like it when you say things
and you mean them. Cosas como
'no,' 'I don't care,' and 'ya.'
As if you want to go into another world.

Yo recuerdo when you were chiquitito:
you would eat tomatoes with picatitos
that wore away el piel,
chunky jugo trickling out.

You would never talk,
masticando tomatoes to the center,
never blinking, a stain of pulp roja
remained around tu cheeks y teeth.

Nunca did you make efforts to clean it off,
so I leaned in to wipe your face
and I would laugh and smile and say
mi niño, niño mío.

NOCHES KEMAH | QUESTIONS WITH ANSWERS

can shrimp whiskers grow longer than themselves?

we pinch their heads off
& pile the grey bodies.

how do gold coins sink into a mirror?

this unsheathes shivering onyx
underneath everything's shell.

when does that night road converge into an eclipse?

his eyes shut to hear a boy sitting on seawall ruins singing
el hoyo de mi alma será lleno con los tragos de tu amor years ago.

will a switchblade become lodged in a whale's belly?

hermit crabs abandon
one home for another.

why do concrete's exposed veins glow rust red at midnight?

la luz de tu cariño es un fragmento
en el mar de mi tristeza.

BEING HIGH IN A MOVIE THEATER ON WESTHEIMER IS MY AMERICA

tracking shots   of broken teeth
kaleidoscope my   phantom skin
when i remember to look up
they're talking about   a bomb
in someone's country   to be dealt with
as a metaphor   for how   perfect
an empire's engine   percolates   wait
all the characters   are played by one
white actor   switching wigs &
inflating lips   mid-scene   using
CGI   the sidekick   is someone's
tío in a canary body   crooning   *you're*
right, compadre™   hold up
that's different   that's an insurance commercial
from 2002   this guy's different
doing the same voice   playing a villain
who wants revenge   his origin story   is
"America took   everything   from me"
cut to   the ripe bomb resting   in the womb
of a red school   "he's taking this too far"   the white actor
responds   while staring at my empty hands   this
is too obvious   I mean   there's even a scene
where the white actor says they don't see   brown, black,
white, blue, purple, blurple   i already can't
remember how the movie ends   it's ok
i'll daydream it later   because right now
i have to not fall down some stairs
i leave my seat   pebbles of stars
blink me to an exit   like i'm leaving
an orientation   to enter an afterlife
now to pick the correct   door
by the time   the lobby lens flares me
i realize   the movie   hadn't ended
oh fuck i'm too embarrassed   to complete
what i paid for

my eyes panoramic   & focus on a family
not mine   but very much mine   in a sitcom
about me   the child pulls their mother
to a poster   for a movie   about a laughing dog
played by   that white actor   the mom reminds him
"y si dios   quiere"   which translates to
"I will give it   everything I have   but there's a plan
we aren't   a part of yet"   the child then leads her
to a coal-eyed robot   convulsing with edible doubloons
please let my psychopomp   be so generous   as to guide me
to my eternity   by the hand   in a humming stroll
like this child navigating   the legal sugars   of a concession
stand   & not along   a path of throat singing rocks
lit by electric veins   echoing from a screaming vortex
i'm about to be tossed into   for savoring sins
i was notified of   well in advance   in writing
i ask someone   for water   who informs me
of an apparatus   over there   that miracles it   by
pushing a lever   with a paper cup   i hate
being this vulnerable in public   that someone will
see me for myself   & ask   "are you ok?"
the accurate answer is   it's complicated
since there comes a time   in a man's life   when he
reaches 30   something he didn't think   possible
at 20   overdrinking beer   as bitter as gunpowder
he was supposed to be buried in   duh   i'm that man
the real question is   "if this is a nation of tradition
how are you not   its catchphrase?"   to which i'll slur
"i drink & love & surrender at my own expense"
which is about   half true   when i finally
finish the movie   it will have won several awards

D. THE CITY IS EL COSMOS

THE FIRST MEXICAN AMERICAN ASTRONAUT WAS ONCE

a child lost in a field at night

world turns
on an axis
a baby feels
mother's nipple

standing lonely
in this pelagic field

rip sugar beets, lettuce,
cucumbers, tomatoes
from their dirt birth

place them in baskets
to be sold

wipe hurting wet
from night-blind eyes

look upward & see
sesame seeds in mole

in this dream
become so lost
amongst looming crops

raise your arms
in surrender for direction

scrape porfa
from pumiced gullet

beg the god of stardust & loam
to relieve this finality

renounce the body
water be thy blood
heart a fist of seeds
dirt the lineage of skin

the mind is cacti under
air-gulping sun

stalks whisper
their nonsense

miralo, every migrant
a star shooting
towards fulfillment

there's no such thing as home
merely space to build life
love what you must until death

believing otherwise is a coward's lie
you, lesser than god, entiende
your life is borrowed time

your home is borrowed space
to make others more subject
to this truth is the first & final sin

wake up huddled
in a puddle
color of the moon

unfold your arms skyward
a star flutters, flatlines
then vanishes just like that

i've been wandering ever since

on tv as another version of himself

a white line fattens
at the television's belly
that enunciates half
words when struck
on the side & garbles
with a mouth full
of ants swarming
on steel wool but
        he's there on that
        cauliflower moon,
        the astronaut who
        reminds me of me.

the astronaut's face
collapses on itself
like a dying spider's
dying limbs. i skew
the antenna's arms
until there's a man
thousands of miles
outside my planet
in the tv. the sole thing
closer to the situation
is the moon itself.
        i can see my apparition
        years from now through
        a spit hole in the jet fuel sky.

when no one
believes me i cry
so hard i'm hiccups
in a boy suit. to feel
the moon's cheek on
my bare skin, i stretch
rabbit ears to their limit while
a facsimile of a man stepping
off an alloyed craft onto
plátano meat develops
upside down. i'm qualified
to be led by my ambitions.

    before bed, i ask "you ready
    for me up there gordo?"
    the moon winks.
    its iris is my
    thumbprint.

a man soused in anti-gravity

floating in the sky above the sky // the stars are even further away // oye what you try to reach may have // already become a memory // i was once a child who ripped colors // from the earth // now i am a man of one mind // floating above us all // in zero gravity utero // what difference is this to any god? // si, la tierra is blue green brown // a machine tells me nothing hurts // i don't want facts simply the truth // i look down at the planet // & translate its topography // for the answer before my question // the mountains read // "this line is a line is a line is a line // a line is drawn for comfort // there's nothing wrong with this // until someone draws a line for you // look upon this skin // you'll find no lines // yet people die every day // for what is not there // to make others more subject // to this illusion is the first & final sin // how does one escape lines? // in the face of such quandary // i am nothing & i am matter // what is a body really? // what does this body mean? // am i both? am i neither? // am i me? am i a people? // am i a nation? am i the earth? // i look down again at the turning tierra // i re-witness sharkskin abyss // nothing's clear to me // i'm ok with this // is no one else?

on another planet with another species

Here they worship water, its ability
to fit any container, how each drop
is its own conscious, the way it wads
up, dances, & vapors off a hot skillet.
When someone cries, there's a bottling
ritual to repurpose the tears– sobs
of sadness for cooking, weeps of happiness
to anoint. I teach them the words: 'water.
agua. H2O.' They teach me to draw symbols
on my arms with water & study their
evaporation, their form of prayer. They build
glass monuments, glass cathedrals, glass
sculptures, glass symbols on glass walls in glass
homes & fill each structure with water.
Every so often, they'll destroy them, melt
the shards down, & build them anew to be filled
with more water as per a scripture that must
constantly be rewritten on sheets of scalding
iron with water that dervishes on impact.
They were horrified to learn that our vast rivers
of speaking water act as borders, which I explained
were artificial designations of geopolitics based
on the results of historical events. They tell me
doom awaits such a people & explain
how they place their most esteemed dead
in a coffin of ice pushed down a river that empties
into an ocean. I am too tired to explain the rest.

someone who forgot he was back on earth

i close my eyes & open
them as someone walking
on some celestial body.

the floor is made of scorpion
scales & reflect galaxis, an eye
of onyx blinking in a pool of oil.

no sound, not even breathing
or thoughts. my sightline
converges upon an axis

that supernovas & approaches.
my teeth gorge. my feet exhale.
a prickling begins at my ankles.

a freighter of pulsing light nears.
a star rises up my spine. an
ambulance of bullet-sharp light

fragments me with thickening
vibrations. my eyes crystallize. heat
dissipates from my silt throat & off

my glass tongue. i scream until
my lungs spaghettify. i accept
this. upon completion, they name me

according to my shape: ojo de caballo.
the bathroom mirror conjures my visage.
when i touch my face, my reflection

laughs. i'm already a memory of myself.
when i caress my cheek, my hands taste
a cold wall. defining immateriality has value.

a boy dying as another version of himself

carbon monoxide loots
his organs of their oxygen
& what he feels is a day light
weaving fever between
cilia of wheat.
                    a veces, es lo
que pasa. i asked my father
how one survives in america,
& he spat in the dirt. "finish
your work before it evaporates
o la tierra te tragara, niño."

there's a version of me
that couldn't do this
which is to say there's
a version of you singing
on a mountain.
                    i imagine
i'm not meant to see this
since i can't reach in &
remove him from this fate
which is to say we're a city
of bones on seafloor, too.

someone who forgot he was on the moon

i see earth as one

horse eye saturated

blue turning in its grave.

clouds are axolotl shadows

dragging bellies & tails

across a lake bottom.

the lens socket of a hurricane

magnifies the violence driven

by each of its fingers.

i'll teach us all

to collapse inward

& leap like seedheads.

each burial contributes

to harvesting our heat death

& there are no borders.

someone who remembered he was back on earth

a velvet matter   b l a n k e t s
the horse eye's surface   i t s v o i d
enters our feet   snakes up our g u t s
fills us   to the dented p i t
of our palates   e v a c u a t e s
out our vacant gums   as phosphene m a c h e t e s
that join   into l o n g s o n g
cleaving   e a r t h

LOS REYES | THAT DREAM

"And being warned of God in a dream that they should not return [...], they departed into their own country [...]."
Matthew 2:12

El Rey of Ghosts

The living & the dead
omit the absent. A country
of wandering,
wonder before definition.
Smoke escaping fire. Weapon
painting wound.
Children are cast from their home.
A tree cracks knife-thin across
its belly & fractures
into lightning. The mouth singing
the river of cumin home
chokes on honey & glass.

El Rey of First Breaths

A kingdom with three
kings is a question
with no answer.
Grief the size of a gold tooth
splits down its radian
& emits cumin.
A glob of amber holds a cracked
seed. A birth glimmers along
the horizon like motor oil
dripping from a stinger. The boy's ghost
swims sunward in a sea of glass
siphoning into an eclipse.

El Rey of Gold Teeth

Nations of day & night
converge skins, igniting
a river of gold teeth
with cumin & sea glass
at its banks. Twilight
indulges liminality.
A breath before a kiss.
The sip of water punctuating
a thirst. A vision resulting
in revelation. Ghosts wilt to their
foreheads as quicksand drinks
song notes leading home.

ANSWERS WITHOUT QUESTIONS

for Rosemary Casals

00:03:46.00 - 00:3:53.10
I had no idols. Think: at a dinner table,
a blue bowl reflects your face

00:3:53.10 - 00:03:58.96
as a drowning angel. stomach scream-
speaking, do you think about rosemary-

00:03:58.96 - 00:04:05.44
licked crust of roasted chicken crackling
between your teeth & wait for someone

00:04:05.44 - 00:04:12.24
to deliver this fantasy? no. you leave
& prepare a feast from your ambitions.

00:04:12.25 - 00:04:38.31

00:04:38.32 - 00:04:49.34
There's no such thing as strength, just
what survives restraint. why don't you

00:04:49.34 - 00:04:59.89
ask a caged motmot about the
possibilities of its turquoise wings?

00:04:59.89 - 00:05:10.96
the impossibilities of the pendulous
black rackets at tail's end? To answer

00:05:10.96 - 00:05:17.03
your question, it's my movement &
overhead, how I'm seen yet inconceivable,

00:05:17.03 - 00:05:21.28
how I smack a ball in-
to its fate, respectively.

00:05:21.29 - 00:05:31.80

00:05:31.80 - 00:05:39.59
I can prevaricate with words like dedication,
heart, & discipline, but truly, it takes

00:05:39.59 - 00:05:47.84
everything: a willingness to be inspected
like a crime scene; able to answer someone

00:05:47.84 - 00:05:55.85
calmly when they ask if you belong here;
the desire to transform the tennis ball into a

00:05:55.85 - 00:06:02.51
whirling sun; and being ready for all
of it to never be enough.

00:06:02.51 - 00:07:00.00

00:07:00.00 - 00:07:11.61
No one memory ever defines a life. That's like
seeing one frame to experience a film.

00:07:11.61 - 00:07:19.03
When you think about it, death is when
an object or moment or person

00:07:19.03 - 00:07:29.43
is removed of its story. Sans history & future,
a thing is just a thing, an heirloom with no

00:07:29.43 - 00:07:36.78
heir. Let me put it this way: I've lost everything
but won everything, as well.

00:07:36.78 - 00:07:43.14
Really, I'm everything & its loss, the loss
& everything's return.

00:07:43.15 - 00:07:48.43

00:07:48.43 - 00:07:55.89
If you're about it, you always want to play
the best. If I could play against god,

00:07:55.89 - 00:08:02.02
then I'd play against god. Not that I'm foolish enough
to think I could beat god, but I

00:08:02.02 - 00:08:07.38
just want to know how god would play, how
potent the serves would be, how the ball

00:08:07.38 - 00:08:16.03
would exist outside the bounds of time & space,
how even god will respect that

00:08:16.03 - 00:08:25.05
what they give, I will return,
& what I give, they will accept.

HOT CHIP PRAYER

crumbs of the sun
morsels of chispas
puffs of hard blood
portrait heavy gore
on each dedo & uvula
load through our teeth
like bullets into chambers
beads along a palm
sabor de picas
force us to huff in & out
our creature maws
swell the insides
of our cheeks, line
our drool with rage
red spit slaps
the hot sidewalk
the new heart dulls
into its shadow
our stomachs
& intestines blush
the hue of violence
porfa let us
indulge
to escape
the earth's
turn

THE FABULOUS WONDROUS OUTFITS OF THE FABULOUS WONDER TWINS

"I Will Survive," Diana Ross, 1996 (1:36)

what grief in this home has been made again? the schools empty. the blackboards clean. the art in museums alone, & the dozing guards nowhere to be found. supermarket shelves bereft, & their sickly lights reveal nada. a government fails, & its citizens now all orphans. a throbbing anthill curdles necropolis grey & topples by this summer's end. i've once left behind my one body in a bed of sweat & saw myself in open-eyed awe. i left behind my one home & saw the lights on but no phantasmagoric splendor of life.

i leapt into the one sky, looking down at an earth of the tops of heads: pastel polka dots roaming the fuschia spandex of twilight's glow on an evening earth. who does not wish this spotted world's shoulders wrapped in a coat? why not make this coat's color the pink of mammalian birth? why not endow this coat's skin with the fur of an alien animal? why not wear it out to a club & dance in celebration of the air, the water, the breathing & drinking of joy through one mouth? why not? why not? why not?

FROM A PHOTO BOOTH AT GREENSPOINT MALL

is surveillance-gray footage of a little brother & big sister smushed cheek to cheek, the pixels around their dimples grainy as gravel, fingers v-signed, proof of any relation in their bestowed mother's lips that would be belly-pink like the innards of conches had the technology been accessible to colorize this 8.5x11" monument to an afternoon whim of wandering among facades, sipping from a shared cup of strawberry soda & never affording any shoes or books. but yes, $4.95 to make timeless timelessness, just focus eyes camera-ward, follow the hollow underside of a ziggurat cascading into a peephole silvering with potential. hold that breath, invoke a smile, be still a moment, be a people in an x-large Looney Toons shirt

or black tank top & bleached jeans, tattooed eyeliner, blonde highlighted hair, mauve mouthed & dark necked, as though later the big sister will drive a poppy red sedan that clunks up concrete freeways, radio singing nuhnah nuhnah & the little brother will too. a giggle. a sigh. a bulb ignites. an eye shuts. oxygen becomes carbon dioxide again. what could not be done in color can be expressed by adding stickers (a cartoon heart, birds chewing ribbon, clouds, a rainbow) framing two faces conjoined by shadow. neither sibling blinked, so there's four pupils staring at what must be a version of themselves in some other time in some other place from a bent document noting a tenderness in the blood.

THE 73 BUS NEAR BELLFORT AROUND 5:00 P.M. IS MY AMERICA

The cold air hurts twice
   breathing in then out
& every sidewalk is cracked
   I step inside this bus
People rest in steel pews
   The tires sing with strain
The street is an infinite film
   Buildings exist until they don't
There's no need to look
   in someone else's eyes
This bus is a nation of waiting
   I sit & become its citizen

At the next stop, 10 Black & Brown mothers
   with their children
join this nation too
   but every seat is full
The tired sigh all at once
   & rise to their feet
The main unspoken law is
   no mother or child shall suffer
within their waiting
   The second silence
This is America absolutely
   but no one here shall be its victim

I stand & a mother settles down
   with a child in her lap
How grand to witness
   this altar of the primordial love
between creator & creation
   I surrender to its peace
& find comfort in my irrelevance
   Let anyone that disrupts this
milagro be buried in hot sand
   the ashes left to nourish
the growth of their enemy
   I am 23 stops away from my exile

The passage of time has a call tone
   & hangs through a bus engine
that becomes part of the air
   We all breathe in its droning
As the bus stops for me
   the brakes scream with purpose
I get off and watch this ferry pass
   No one there will remember me
Every nation is a means
   to an end
This is a nation that completes
   beyond me

A LESSON TOWARDS DISPOSSESSION

My father   as a child
witnessed a country's   death
aiming down   the gas-black horizon
of a gun   longer than a timeline.

My father   as a child
carried an M-16   or an AK-47
as I would lug a green backpack
on an early stroll   to school.

A child   with a gun   is the final wall
at the end   of every imagination.
Can you trust   a reality   that conceived this?
I'm not going to say   any more about it.

My father   as a child
was probably smuggled   into Texas
in a van or trunk   a discrete seed
of desire sown in moonlight.

An escape   grew into a life.
I wouldn't   be here
otherwise. What am I   but a
harvest of   an American fate?

The story is   Salvadoreños
emerged from corn   or from a primordial cave
or who knows   since so many stories
have been lost   in the deep breath of history.

I've been told   by nations   that Salvadoreños
are to be saved   from the guns
we supposedly hold   like paintbrushes
in our masterpiece   of violence.

Does violence flow in   every vein
of every Salvadoreño?   My father
as a child   held a gun.   My father
as a man   prepared mariscadas.

In my hands   is there to be a rifle,
dark as dirt   with blood in it   aimed
at my reflection   to shoot
for no other purpose   than for the shards to rot?

Colonization   is a pedagogy
I master with every   envisioning
of my destruction.   What is the mind
but a container   of spilled sangre?

Pues, no rifle here.   What I cannot read
I interpret with ink   a paper   lines
between lines   emptiness   the capacity
for   my language

NOTES

The poem "The First Mexican American Astronaut Was Once on tv as another version of himself" contains lines inspired by the last lines of Rita Dove's "The Zeppelin Factory."

The poem "The First Mexican American Astronaut Was Once a man soused in anti-gravity" contains remixed lines from Gertrude Stein and William Carlos Williams.

The poem "The First Mexican American Astronaut Was Once on another planet with another species" was inspired by F.J. Bergmann's poem "Hydromorphology" in the chapbook *A Catalogue of the Further Suns.*

ACKNOWLEDGMENTS

My gratitude to all the editors of the following publications who believed in my work:

Infrarrealista Review: All of "The Fabulous Wondrous Outfits of the Fabulous Wonder Twins." (2021).

december magazine: A version of "Finding Kittens After a Tropical Storm is My America" originally published as "Finding a Kitten Behind an Air Conditioner After a Tropical Storm is my America." (2021).

Cosmonauts Avenue: "El Salvadoreño Americano as Decolonizer, 1929-1936." (2020).

december magazine (2018) & *BreakBeat Poets* vol. 4: LatiNEXT. (2020): "Eddie Guerrero Enters a Ring Holding the World Championship."

What's the New News? Issue 3: A version of "A 4th Grade Dance Party in a Cafeteria at 1p.m. is My America" originally published as "A 4th Grade Dance Party in the Cafeteria on a Monday at 1p.m. in Houston is My America." (2019).

Tule Review: A version of "A Broken Red-Eared Slider's Shell" originally published as "The Red Eared Slider." (2019).

Palabritas: A version of "A Lesson in Dispossession" originally published as "A Portrait of my Father, the Child Soldier, & Me, the Writer." (2019).

pariahs anthology: writing from outside the margins (2016) & Houston Public Media (2019): "Selena's Last Concert in Houston."

Gulf Coast Journal: Sections of "Hijo, please." (2017).

Origins Literary Journial: A version of "A Gospel of a New America" originally published as "The Gospel of Carlos Cienfuegos." (2016).

I wish to thank my family, without whom poetry is just words: Romeo, Allyza, Angelica, Veronica, Ricky, and mi mama.

I wish to thank my new family, who crafted the best poem that continues to inspire me every day: Retta, Daisy, Marcia, and Nora.

I wish to thank the love of my life: Robyn.

I wish to thank Eduardo C. Corral, who pushed me to be the best poet I could ever be, before he even knew me.

I wish to thank Rigoberto González, who believed in me and my work enough to set me on my journey of published books and dreams.

I wish to thank Sarah Rafael García, who was there when I needed her most and continues to teach me.

I wish to thank my community, friends, writers, artists, organizers, and educators who have inspired and supported me throughout my life. There are so, so many names in so many places that I get dizzy thinking of all of them, scared that I'll miss someone (and you always do). What a blessing. You know who you are. I'll hit you up in a bit. I love you.

I wish to thank the Hub City Press team, who circled back and brought me in and made this something you can hold in your hands: Meg Reid, Kate McMullen, Katherine Webb-Hehn, and Julie Jarema.

I wish to thank you. Yes, you.

PUBLISHING
New & Extraordinary
VOICES FROM THE
AMERICAN SOUTH

HUB CITY PRESS is a non-profit independent press in Spartanburg, SC that publishes well-crafted, high-quality works by new and established authors, with an emphasis on the Southern experience. We are committed to high-caliber novels, short stories, poetry, plays, memoir, and works emphasizing regional culture and history. We are particularly interested in books with a strong sense of place.

Hub City Press is an imprint of the non-profit Hub City Writers Project, founded in 1995 to foster a sense of community through the literary arts. Our metaphor of organization purposely looks backward to the nineteenth century when Spartanburg was known as the "hub city," a place where railroads converged and departed.

RECENT HUB CITY PRESS POETRY

In the Hands of the River • Lucien Darjeun Meadows

Thresh & Hold • Marlanda Dekine

Reparations Now! • Ashley M. Jones

Sparrow Envy: A Field Guide to Birds and Lesser Beasts • J. Drew Lanham

Cleave • Tiana Nobile

Mustard, Milk, and Gin • Megan Denton Ray

Dusk & Dust • Esteban Rodriguez

Rodeo in Reverse • Lindsey Alexander

Magic City Gospel • Ashley M. Jones

Wedding Pulls • J.K. Daniels